Releasing

Bilingual Press/Editorial Bilingüe

General Editor
Gary D. Keller

Managing Editor
Karen S. Van Hooft

Associate Editors
Ann Waggoner Aken
Theresa Hannon

Assistant Editor
Linda St. George Thurston

Editorial Consultant
Janet Woolum

Editorial Board
Juan Goytisolo
Francisco Jiménez
Eduardo Rivera
Severo Sarduy
Mario Vargas Llosa

Address:
Bilingual Review/Press
Hispanic Research Center
Arizona State University
Box 872702
Tempe, Arizona 85287-2702
(602) 965-3867

Releasing Serpents

Bernice Zamora

Bilingual Press/Editorial Bilingüe
TEMPE, ARIZONA

ublication may by reproduced in
riting, except in the case of brief
s and reviews.

ı-Publication Data

Releasing serpents : poems / Bernice Zamora.
    p.   cm.
    ISBN 0-927534-39-8 (pbk.)
    1. Mexican American women—Poetry. I. Title.
PS3576.A45R4   1993
811'.54—dc20   93-11946
                                                      CIP

PRINTED IN THE UNITED STATES OF AMERICA

Cover design by Kerry Curtis
Cover art by José Antonio Burciaga
Back cover photo by Susan Bradley

Acknowledgments

Major new marketing initiatives have been made possible by the Lila
Wallace-Reader's Digest Literary Publishers Marketing Develop-
ment Program, funded through a grant to the Council of Literary
Magazines and Presses.

Funding provided by a grant from the National Endowment for the
Arts in Washington, D.C., a Federal agency.

The quoted lines in the poems "California," "Pico Blanco," and " 'The
Extraordinary Patience of Things' " are from the poems "Roan Stal-
lion," "Return," "To Death," "The Inquisitors," "Cassandra," and
"Carmel Point" by Robinson Jeffers, from *Selected Poems* (New York:
Random House, 1965).

Acknowledgments continue on p. 116.

CONTENTS

Bernice Zamora:
Self and Community

Nancy Vogeley
University of San Francisco

In putting pen to paper, Chicana writers have acted to create their own identity in the world of literature.[1] In an essay published in 1979 Judy Salinas described three Chicana types who, she said, reflect the universal feminine types inhabiting the imaginative world of mainstream literatures: the good woman (Mary), the bad woman (Eve), and the woman less frequently seen but whose image, on a more realistic level, mixes the two.[2] She saw Chicano literary production, even of male authors, as tending to blur the distinctions between the principal types and consequently to avoid moral absolutes. Recent Chicana writing, however, such as that contained in the 1990 volume *Making Face, Making Soul/Haciendo caras: Creative and Critical Perspectives by Feminists of Color*,[3] insists that Chicanas must speak for themselves; in fact, various essays in this volume assume an even more aggressive stance in calling for women to remove their masks in a rebellion against racism and sexism.

What from one perspective is seen as the shedding of masks, the discarding of inauthenticity and posing for others, from another, however, may be interpreted as a process of turning inward. Marcienne Rocard has written perceptively that "since the mid-seventies . . . unlike the men of their community, who could afford to be unself-centered, they [Chicanas] have made self-reflexion the first priority" (130-131).[4] To prove her point Rocard cites works by Virginia Cantú, Carrie A. Castro, Gloria Treviño, Margarita Cota-Cárdenas, Elena Guadalupe Rodríguez, Marcela Lucero-Trujillo, Estela Portillo Trambley, Lorna Dee Cervantes, Lydia Camarillo, Isabel Ríos, Inés Hernández Tovar, and Bernice Zamora.

1

Introspection, however, can carry dangers, as Juan Rodríguez has shown in an important essay, "La búsqueda de identidad y sus motivos en la literatura chicana."[5] In this study based on Chicano authors, Rodríguez sees that "un yoísmo pernicioso [puede] dar cabida a héroes románticos . . . o héroes existencialistas" (175-176). He finds in Chicano literature a frequent flight from present-day realities to a closed, mythical past, one which assumes that the Chicanos' material problems are already solved. Rodríguez understands that the present search for identity undertaken by Chicano poets, artists, and intellectuals is similar to those searches of bourgeois thinkers who, since the Industrial Revolution, have struggled with the alienation and personal frustration that political and economic forces unleashed. However, rather than emphasizing the universality of this experience, Chicanos, he believes, must situate their self-awareness in a consciousness of difference from the "other," in a critical confrontation of their "condición de dominado" and their internalization of ruling-class values.

David T. Abalos, in his discussion of the transformation of Latino society in the United States, provides an extended commentary on the suppressed anger of Latinos, which manifests itself in passivity, fatalism, and silence; he criticizes the invasion of the self that assimilation usually entails.[6] He, like Rodríguez, defines the Latino self in terms of social relationships, for the most part traditionally those of the family and the Church. Interestingly, Abalos repeats Rodríguez's warning that narcissism in the male's frequent experience of love is an attempt, which is often frustrated, to recreate an image of power he has created for himself (69).

Salvador Rodríguez del Pino discusses "las poetisas chicanas" in an important early (1979) attempt to mark the emergence of these writers and to give a historical context to their effort to wrest an identity for Chicanas as a double minority.[7] He writes that their poetry takes as its subject matter both the oppression by the larger system and the oppression by Chicano machismo inherited, he believes, from Mexican culture.

2

Bernice Zamora occupies a curious place in the development of Chicano letters. In his description of her work Rodríguez del Pino includes her in his discussion of major male poets with the explanation: "Bernice Zamora ha tenido la distinción o el dudable halago de que su poesía 'parece haber sido escrita por un hombre' " (86). Although he does not elaborate on the meaning of this assertion, the reader concludes that because Zamora does not dwell nostalgically on barrio scenes, does not handle her female subordination with either sweet resignation or bitterness, but does produce a style which is "pulida y calculada," her poetry is somehow more male. This attempt by Rodríguez del Pino to sort out cultural expectations for gender-based types of writing is a helpful signpost that I will return to later.

In her 1986 volume on Chicano poetry Cordelia Candelaria makes Zamora the representative of "the stylized Phase III poetry written by Chicanas in the mid-1970s" (170).[8] Candelaria here is trying to construct a chronology in which social-protest poetry related to the Movement (Phase I) is followed by evolving techniques and themes represented primarily by Alurista's first two books (Phase II). She defines Phase III in this way: "Phase III poetry features a polarity describable as subject-I versus object-Other" (137). The "multilingualism, *mestizaje,* and ritual" of Phase II have given way to "stylistic skill and lyrical subtlety" and "a multiplicity of subjects and themes that range beyond . . . *raza* concerns" (137-8). Two poets—Gary Soto and Bernice Zamora—represent for her the achievement of "a private, highly subjective, personal voice" (138). Candelaria's identification here of an I-Other polarity as important to the works of this period is a point I will also return to later.

Bernice Zamora was born January 28, 1938, in Aguilar, a small town in the coal-mining region of Colorado, a state whose population was a mixture of Chicanos, Italians, Slovenians, and Anglo-Texans, and where she stayed until after she was married.[9] When asked once about her forebears, she traced her ancestry back to immigrant Spaniards and resident Indians, and then, revealingly, repented of the statement because, she said, "tracing one's genealogy is an exercise in arrogance," one which is often used against Chicanos.

Zamora's family spoke a "vernacular English" at home although Spanish was used with grandparents. Zamora has described how she taught herself to read from cereal boxes, how her knowledge surprised the nuns when at the age of three she was taken to catechism class along with the older children so that her mother might be free. She has said that as a child, she "had a passion for school and studies, for doing good and escape." However, she continued:

> Life was one full shock after another; and it is painful for me to speak of childhood experiences. One of the reasons I write today is that these experiences left me with a shyness and such a timidity, it was nearly impossible to express myself vocally, verbally, or even by actions, except in school. [10]

Until the eighth grade Zamora attended Catholic schools and "aspired to be a nun the whole time." In the community at large, it was frowned upon to use Spanish publicly; thus, she was educated in English and used the language predominantly. She speaks of the delight she experienced when she finally saw, written down, the Spanish words she had only heard.

In high school she took business subjects and showed an aptitude for art. She worked for a bank for a while, married, and had two daughters. She continued to read and also took classes at night. At that time she read the works of Kierkegaard and Sartre, although, she has said, without understanding a great deal. One night, however, at an auxiliary meeting for women of the Knights of Columbus, she was stunned when another woman, the mother of eight, mentioned existentialism. When Zamora asked her where she had learned about philosophy and the woman replied that she had been taking classes at night, Zamora decided that she too could study seriously.

4

At the age of 28 she enrolled at Southern Colorado University and in three years earned a B.A. degree in French and English. She went on to complete an M.A. degree at Colorado State in Fort Collins in 1972. There she continued her interests in French and English and wrote a thesis on the poetry of Francis Ponge and Wallace Stevens. Increasingly, she was becoming aware of the different approaches to thinking which each literature represented; in the study of French literature, for example, she found more freedom, more careful examination of texts, and more opportunity to study women writers than in the British tradition. Although she liked Shakespeare (a play of his, she has said, would "spin me on to writing about twelve poems"), she was "absolutely enthralled" with Dante and considered many non-English writers superior to most British authors. Through the study of literature, she came to an understanding of being "divided," of being bicultural, and at this time she began to write her own poetry.

Zamora's troubled marriage ended in 1974 after a year at Marquette University, where she had begun the doctoral program. She does not, however, attribute its end to her decision to continue her education. The other women in her old auxiliary circle, even though they criticized the women's movement then forming, had helped her to think about her life as a wife and a Catholic and, to some extent, supported her growth and questioning attitudes.

She drove west with her two daughters to begin her doctoral studies at Stanford University; she completed her degree in English and American literatures there in 1986. Her dissertation focussed on theoretical questions of Chicano literature. During this period Zamora worked hard to support her family; she taught at Stanford, the University of California at Berkeley, and the University of San Francisco. She wrote and published a great deal. A paper she read at the 1976 meeting of the Modern Language Association, "Archetypes in Chicana Poetry," which was later printed in *De Colores* (1978), determined much of her later critical thinking and poetic practice, as well as that of others. She was active in the Chicano Movement in many ways. In 1980 she and José Armas edited an anthology of Chicano literature from the Flor y Canto festivals held in Albuquerque (1977) and in Tempe, Arizona (1978). In December 1979 Zamora left Stanford for Albuquerque to help edit the journal *De Colores*. In 1980 while in Houston working with Chicanas, she fell desperately ill. In December 1982 she returned to California, and around this time she began to withdraw from her involvement in Chicano activities and to discontinue public appearances. Partly for reasons of health, partly to avoid contention (in her remarks about the work of others, she has been unfailingly generous), partly weary of the academic experience, she declared her future lay outside critical practice and the university. After she completed her doctoral work, she went to Mexico to write and work on some notions about La Malinche. However, she has returned to university teaching at Santa Clara University, where she is today.

The present volume is Bernice Zamora's long-awaited second book. *Restless Serpents,* her first book, evoked a great response when it was published in 1976; for example, Bruce-Novoa said that it "put its author among the leading figures in Chicano literature" (170).[11] In a review of *Restless Serpents,* Lorna Dee Cervantes declared that Zamora, "as evidenced by her tight, carefully crafted poems, proves herself to be one of the most (if not *the* most) outstanding Chicana poets today."[12] Critics have generally remarked on the collection's maturity, noting how Zamora somehow combined folkloric remembrances, political consciousness, and academic concerns.[13] The image of the snake in the title poem and in other poems of the collection suggested to critics the poet's journey to retrieve the Chicano past; Elizabeth J. Ordóñez wrote, for example, that Zamora was engaging in "a process of mythopoesis" as she created identity anew in her poetry.[14] Since 1976, however, apart from the publication of a very few, mostly reprinted, poems, articles, and short stories (and nothing since 1985), Zamora has kept silent, thus tantalizing her readers. During this time, however, she has been exercising her talents. The 30 new poems published here for the first time, as well as much other work she has chosen not to publish to date, represent her development over a period of some 15 years. As of 1990, she estimated that she was writing approximately a poem a day; thus, we can estimate that her unpublished work is considerable.

Because it is difficult (and ultimately of little importance) to separate the poems by date of composition, it will not be my intent to pick out any pattern of change from her earlier to her most recent poetry. Instead I will use the combined collection to argue for an enduring preoccupation of Zamora—a sense of self based on a heightened consciousness of the community for which she is writing. Her poems, in combining self and social realities, avoid the pitfalls of narcissism that Rodríguez and Abalos have pointed out with regard to the Hispanic male. As her poems center on that fine line between the individual and the world outside, they offer important examples of Chicano creativity using literature to buttress the collective self.

Zamora has spoken and written of the importance of poetry reading in her life and career, of her meaningful participation in artistic events such as the Flor y Canto festivals. In several interviews she has emphasized the need to give voice to experiences that Chicana women and others have enjoyed and suffered. She has clarified her feelings about her work as a contribution to a developing culture whose young people are thirsty for texts.

This consciousness of poetry, of shared experience, and of her own work, I believe, translates into her poetry in several ways. The first is perhaps the most obvious. Through her sense of self, she examines relationships and external features of personhood in such a way that factors of race, gender, historical heritage, faith and religion, language, and regional identity frequently enter into her thematics. In *Restless Serpents* this sense of community took the form of recollections of town members, familiar surroundings, family, and adolescence ("Progenitor," "Penitents," and "Plainview" are examples). It also took form in poems in Spanish (such as "A tropezones en Stanford"), in the code switching poems in Spanish and English (such as "Antón Chico Bridge"), and in those poems in English in which the fit between English and Spanish is shown to be awkward or impossible ("Let the Giants Cackle" and "El Burrito Café"). It is also seen in an overlooked poem written for César Chávez, "The Sovereign," whose first line, "Behold the man," recalls the suffering Christ and whose verses describe the world's efforts to classify the work of this man "ignoring / the scheme to usurp him."

In the new poems this consciousness appears transmuted into a self-consciousness based on the poet and her work.[15] Here, unlike the "Arte poética" poems of writers like Pablo Neruda in which the poet's task is conceived of as naming the ineffable, Zamora displays in a poem like "The Chasm" a strong moral sense of herself as taking risks and arguing with God so as to feed the "chicks within the nest." Here she sees herself as drawing near God, as a bird that flies between the earth and the sky; however, unlike the romantic poets who were elevated, it was thought, by their creative genius and special sensitivity to a kind of feeling accepted in the nineteenth century as a substitute for the religious experience, Zamora soars compelled by her own intellectual demands as well as a maternal concern for others. In "The Chasm" she retains the traditional vocabulary of faith in naming God and recalling the Christian symbol of the pelican who pecked open her breast to provide food for her young. In "Letter" she surprisingly groups herself with "priests, / popes and poets"—"None other [she says] particularly concern themselves / beyond the word, the letter." The juxtaposition is curious because the poet is perhaps mockingly, but also perhaps seriously, associated here with institutional mediators between God and individual lives.

The second way in which I see her particular kind of selfhood emerging is through her special sense of the moment. French symbolist poets wrote of the gazing eye and recorded the evidence of the senses, such as sound and color; Spanish poets of this century, too, such as Jorge Guillén, rhapsodized about the plenitude of the moment. Zamora values the moment differently, I think, because of her awareness of how poetry often works in her life and in the lives of the people in the community she knows. She redefines literary practice in light of Chicano expectations for poetry in such a way that its associations with song and music, its message designated for many listeners at once (surmounting barriers of wealth and privilege which divide audiences for poetry in other cultures), convey a strong sense of the poet in union with others. The readings, the festivals, the songs, the *pachangas*—all are performance situations in which poetry's words must work orally and naturally. The intensity of the moment can be increased by a consciousness of the poem's present-oriented time and the clarity of one focus. The imagistic poems, such as the haiku-like "After Image," are examples of this poetic inspiration.

The sense of the moment is also strong in "Luciano," where memories of a dead uncle intrude upon the observation of a lunar eclipse. Sound then takes over with his description:

He was a farmer, a coal miner and then a grave digger.
A look of permanent shock stocked his face, stooped his frame.
Life had lied to him and the truth he bore of that,
bored him into the ground, ground him into a silence,
silenced him with comprehension and incomprehension,
daily, to the end.

Repetition of sounds—both consonants and vowels, producing internal rhyme—and even repetition of words convey the message of the sad life of another moon lover and destroy the poet's initial attempt to objectify the moonscape. The contemplating and thoughtful self is constantly interrupted by exterior scenes and stimuli which correct the self and direct it to areas where it would not go alone. A construction similar to that of "Luciano" occurs in "Awaiting Grace," where night sounds direct the poet's imagination to consider conception.

The "I" and its power to witness and record are made apparent in poems like "Sheen" and "Endurance"; this power, however, finally collapses, unable to order the universe as the poet's reason and protective instincts might like. The series of seven "Recounting the Day" poems, in which the date is given and the occasion described which apparently inspired each poem, are further examples of this type of poetry.

The third way in which Zamora's poems project an awareness of self and community is a little harder to define. It depends on a sense that Zamora is joining two cultures— one that can be variously described as private, interior, womanly, and communal in the Chicano sense and another that some would label public, academic, intellectual, and male. This second culture, which often lays claim to universality, custodianship of the past, and a special access to truth, is a territory usually dominated by First World, institutionally powerful, white males. Zamora bridges this gap between the two cultures in several ways in her poetry. One example from the poems in *Restless Serpents* is the frequently cited "Sonnet, Freely Adapted"; because the reader has the poem at hand, I will quote only the Shakespeare sonnet which provided the inspiration:

Sonnet 116

Let me not to the marriage of true minds
Admit impediments. Love is not love
Which alters when it alteration finds,
Or bends with the remover to remove:
O, no! it is an ever-fixed mark,
That looks on tempests and is never shaken;
It is the star to every wandering bark,
Whose worth's unknown, although his height be taken.
Love's not Time's fool, though rosy lips and cheeks
Within his bending sickle's compass come;
Love alters not with his brief hours and weeks,
But bears it out even to the edge of doom.
    If this be error and upon me proved,
    I never writ, nor no man ever loved.

Zamora's version, from a woman's point of view, never mentions love. Instead "this weary woman," as she describes herself, calls into question the notion of masculinity and seeks to redefine it; the reader understands the abstractions "Love" and "Time," both important from the masculine point of view, are not pertinent to her experience of contact between the sexes. Her poem counters Shakespeare's suggestion of a relationship constantly threatened by challenges. She shows men engaged in battle with other men, obsessed with mind games that are unwinnable. And her poem's resolution, after the polite reproof of Shakespeare and several statements of what men are not and should not be, shows the poet's tired retreat to "gentle femininity."

Zamora is not spurning sexuality in her poem ("Masculinity is not manhood's realm / Which falters when ground passions overwhelm"), but neither is she making a statement of sexual preference as many might think.[16] I believe her woman's voice here gives witness to many failures; woman, in love as well as in many other endeavors of human activity, is isolated with other women and forced to pick up the pieces of her world. There is no special textual evidence to indicate that Zamora is addressing only Chicanos in this poem, although a criticism of machismo may be understood. Instead, by means of the sonnet pattern and the Elizabethan English, she above all seems to be addressing Shakespeare and the tropes of literature that have imposed themselves perniciously on human lives.

"Parody" may be too strong a word to apply to Zamora's strategy here in taking on a master of British and world literature, a figure usually described as universally admired for his knowledge of human nature. In conforming to the sonnet mode used by Shakespeare, Zamora meets the master on his own formal terms. Her gentle humor does not seek to destroy the male but instead appears to nudge him to accept the woman's point of view. However, in the process, she alters the terms of discourse in such a way that Shakespeare's view of love is altered, if not demolished.

Nevertheless, in one of the new poems, "Natural Rites," Zamora confesses that she is still asking herself Shakespeare-like questions about the nature of love and beauty. Her answer—after experiencing love's "horrors"—is: "I cower before the obstinacies." Her inherited language, therefore, makes her the victim of a set of expectations that others have named. Her academic study of Western religion and historical culture has taught her one system of thought, one rational mode of inquiry, which she has internalized. Her struggle is to take that system and that mode, which world culture has evolved, and try to test them against her own experiences. The result is a poetry in which one part of the self contests with another part of the self, perhaps setting up the tension that Rodríguez del Pino sensed in describing Zamora as a poet whose poetry could be male. It is poetry whose language impresses the reader as "pulida y calculada" as it struggles to free itself from the past and make its meaning clear to others. It is poetry which is political and gender-specific, but it is also poetry in which, because the Chicana self takes on a larger community, the Chicano community itself advances—not to be absorbed into the larger community but to challenge its presuppositions and to improve them.

Notes

[1]For a study of self-representation early in the Chicana emergence into literary practice, see Gloria Velásquez Treviño, "Cultural Ambivalence in Early Chicana Literature," in *European Perspectives on Hispanic Literature in the United States*, ed. Genevieve Fabre (Houston: Arte Público Press, 1988), pp. 140-146.

[2]"The Role of Women in Chicano Literature," in *The Identification and Analysis of Chicano Literature*, ed. Francisco Jiménez (New York: Bilingual Press, 1979), pp. 191-240. See also "The Chicana in Chicano Literature" by Carmen Salazar Parr and Genevieve M. Ramírez in *Chicano Literature. A Reference Guide*, ed. Julio A. Martínez and Francisco A. Lomelí (Westport, CT: Greenwood Press, 1985), pp. 97-107.

[3]Ed. Gloria Anzaldúa (San Francisco: Aunt Lute Foundation, 1990).

[4]"The Chicana: A Marginal Woman," in *European Perspectives,* op. cit., pp. 130-139.

[5]In *The Identification and Analysis of Chicano Literature,* op. cit., pp. 170-178.

[6]*Latinos in the United States. The Sacred and the Political* (Notre Dame: University of Notre Dame Press, 1986).

[7]"La poesía chicana: una nueva trayectoria," in *The Identification and Analysis of Chicano Literature,* ed. Francisco Jiménez (New York: Bilingual Press, 1979), pp. 68-89.

[8]*Chicano Poetry. A Critical Introduction* (Westport, CT: Greenwood Press, 1986).

[9]For the biographical material I rely on my essay on Zamora in *Dictionary of Literary Biography, Chicano Writers. First Series,* Vol. 82, ed. Francisco A. Lomelí and Carl R. Shirley (Detroit: Bruccoli Clark Layman, 1989), pp. 289-294, and on the interviews with Zamora by Bruce-Novoa in *Chicano Authors. Inquiry by Interview* (Austin: University of Texas Press, 1980), pp. 203-218; by Wolfgang Binder in *Partial Autobiographies: Interviews with Twenty Chicano Poets* (Erlangen: Palm & Enke, 1985), pp. v-xviii, 221-229; and by Parul Desai, "Interview with Bernice Zamora, A Chicana Poet," in *Imagine,* 2 (Summer 1985), pp. 26-39.

[10]Personal interview, May 1985. I have interviewed Zamora twice (in May 1985 and November 1990). All quotations have been verified with the author.

[11]"Chicano Poetry," in *Chicano Literature. A Reference Guide,* eds. Julio A. Martínez and Francisco A. Lomelí (Westport, CT: Greenwood Press, 1985).

[12]Review of *Restless Serpents, Mango,* No. 2 (1977), pp. 5-6.

[13]Typical is the study by Bruce-Novoa in *Chicano Poetry. A Response to Chaos* (Austin: University of Texas Press, 1982), pp. 160-184.

[14]"The Concept of Cultural Identity in Chicana Poetry," *Third Woman,* Vol. 2 (1984), pp. 75-82.

[15]See Tey Diana Rebolledo who, in "Soothing Restless Serpents: The Dreaded Creation and Other Inspirations in Chicana Poetry," *Third Woman,* 2, No. 1 (1984), pp. 83-102, perceptively studies the *ars poetica/ars genetica* poems of several Chicana poets.

[16]For alternative readings, see Bruce-Novoa, *Chicano Poetry,* pp. 172-173; Marta Ester Sánchez, *Contemporary Chicana Poetry. A Critical Approach to an Emerging Literature* (Berkeley: University of California Press, 1985), pp. 238-244.

For my beloved grandchildren
Pilar José, Víctor, Yida Ana, and Diego Enrique

Para mis nietitos queridos
Pilo, Vico, Yida y Diego

On Living in Aztlán

PENITENTS

Once each year penitentes in mailshirts
journey through arroyos Seco, Huérfano,
to join "edmanos" at the morada.

Brothers Carrasco, Ortiz, Abeyta
prepare the Cristo for an unnamed task.
Nails, planks and type O blood are set
upon wooden tables facing, it is decreed,
the sacred mountain range to the Southwest.

Within the dark morada average
chains rattle and clacking prayer wheels jolt
the hissing spine to uncoil wailing tongues
of Nahuatl converts who slowly wreath
rosary whips to flog one another.

From the mountains alabados are heard:
"En una columna atado se
halló el Rey de los Cielos,
herido y ensangrentado,
y arrastrado por los suelos."

The irresistible ceremony
beckoned me many times like crater lakes
and desecrated groves. I wished to swim
arroyos and know their estuaries
where, for one week, all is sacred in the valley.

¿A QUE HORA VENDEREMOS TODO?

—for Viola

You tell me I must not bear
More children. Indeed
We agree eight are too many
For this world. You counsel
Me on the fruits of joyful mis-
Conception. You take me aside
To your corner and whisper
 A-B-O-R-T-I-O-N
As though I do not
Recognize the end.

Gracias, anyway, Ciudadano,
My conception is not diminished;
My utility is inutility.
Gracias todo el mundo,
But it is I who claim
Indifference to the world.
It is I who am
Exquisite in nakedness
Against the odds
Of benevolence.

WHEN WE ARE ABLE

When we move from this colony
of charred huts that surround
our grey, wooden, one-room house,
we will marry, querido,
we will marry.

When the stranger ceases to
come in the night to sleep in
our bed and ravish what is yours,
we will marry, querido,
we will marry.

When you are able to walk
without trembling, smile
without crying, and eat without fear,
we will marry, querido,
we will marry.

EL ULTIMO BAILE

Ensangrentada me quedo
a medianoche bailando
en mis pensamientos
en la medianoche
muriendo físicamente
sobre ondas de
aguas coloridas,
esperando la última luna
    roja   mojada
me quedo sola bailando
bailando en mi medianoche
bailando en la medianoche
bailando rumbo a la mar
    de la tranquilidad.

PROGENITOR

I am the padre
who drinks whiskey
until sunup and
who makes love to
my virgin daughter
and her friends.

I am the madre
who stands dazed
before the coffin
of my young son
who shot himself in
his girlfriend's car.

I am the primo
who watched the child
play house with her friends,
then married her
at her own request.

I am the puta
who stands alone
on the grave of a
young man. I am
returning the lilies
he gave me.

I am all the children
and I am the abuelos
of dead children
whose resurrections
depend on
resurrections.

PUEBLO, 1950

I remember you, Fred Montoya.
You were the first vato to ever kiss me.
I was twelve years old.
My mother said shame on you,
my teacher said shame on you, and
I said shame on me, and nobody
    said a word to you

BEARDED LADY

I wanted to know about love
and was told to see the bearded lady.

As she stroked her treasure, she
told me of the melding wells of Julia,

Of the kissing stones shaped
like camels,

Of the hair like linen
found among the cloistered,

And she stroked, and stroked, and stroked

ASUNTO DE PRINCIPIO

Mi amor queda como
prehistoric huesos laying
witness to mujeres salvajes
que viven en silencio,
escondidas, tal vez,
pero con fuerza
dando vueltas a mis huesos,
a mis tesoros que yo les
robo cada noche contigo.

GATA POEM

Desde la cima me llamó
Un hombre perfecto, un chicano
Con cuerpo desnudo y tan moreno que
He glistened in the sun like a bronze god.

—Ven, mujer.
   Ven conmigo.

Se me empezó a morir como una gata
      en la noche.
Y yo misma era gata vestida de negro.

—¿Qué quieres, señor?
   ¿Qué quieres conmigo?

—Quiero cantar eternamente contigo
      lejos de la tristeza.
Quiero enseñarte un sol tan brillante
      que debemos verlo con alma escudada.
Quiero vivir contigo por los nueve mundos.

—Ven, gatita.
   Ven conmigo.

        Y me fui.

ON LIVING IN AZTLAN

—para la familia Arias

We come and we go
But within limits,
Fixed by a law
Which is not ours;

We have in common
the experience of love

after Guillevec

Girded Us

HAVING DROWNED

It is indecent by any standard
to drown and drown again
until the spirit drips assuredly,
absurdly dangling like a hag's rag
to be sopped and wrung and sopped again.

Having drowned, I cannot face the water
to lie flat among lily pads lodged in
frog ponds, nor to lie back awaiting
a caretaker's hook to divide
the drowning from the drowned.

Division is accursed provision.
Resurrecting the drowned is an ogre's task
diminishing to me and other seasoned dead
who reap no glee from the shrinking of the caretaker
in this momentary suspension.

CALIFORNIA

"The night-wind veering, the smell of the spilt wine
drifted down hill from the house."
Two gods lay at my feet; I have
shot one, and that one killed the other.
Each in his turn, each in his fashion of late
laid over me splitting hairs, splitting atoms.
The dog, dead too, leaped to his death.

Beasts they were, both of them beasts—one
of the wind and rein, one of the night and wine
and all of us pools in the moonlight.
My child stands witness to one aimed shot, three
flamed and freeing ones, and one that plunged
my wailing will to the center of this bloody corral.

SUPPING ON . . .

What fools we must seem
to the higher minds of things,
dancing rapturously with ourselves,
by ourselves; eating ravenously
with each other, of each other
and holding up our pebble minds
as gems to be admired by
the pawning apes
of state.

In a stupor we dance
with broad feet, broader
than barefoot paupers,
and think ourselves graceful,
pirouetting to the pawky
feasting tables of uncured
hams, sauce potatoes, and
gallows wine.

We seat ourselves up
on downy cushions
rented for this common
feast. Galvanic us
bound for the larger
goblets; we drink the barm,
and swill our minds
with proper pools of
festing thought.

Drink, drink, drink
to the requins! Sing,

sing, sing to the requins!
Boast, boast, boast of
the swarming fleas!
Ho, ho, ho
to the falstaffs.
Row, row, row
the boat . . .

MORNING AFTER

His mirrored self,
Witness to one chipped
Day or night or both,
Mocks the sorrowed half-
Spent frown. Pallid
Lips, stained from
Grapes now turned to stone,
Purl to breach the
Silence and trembling cheeks.
                He eases
His bulk from fact to fiction—
Bargain, prostitute—one
Mind for one sleep,
Then dreams of one
Chair rocking the
Cliff's edge.

THE SOVEREIGN

—for César Chávez

Behold the man whose
bones are pillars that
sustain the world.
The cosmos is obscured
to a heavy head bent,
but to measure the distance
of the stars is not the work
of a man whose head is directed
toward a heart promiscuous
with love and justice.
Nor is it his desire to pose
for myths like Sisyphus
to be abstracted and hammered
by a fool's tool which nails
soft objects to soft objects
and of little use to the
soul of things.
His stance is foolery
to sentries who think
the world retains the world
unwatched and thriving
of its own volition.
Yet fast he stands, orbed
at the shoulders, ignoring
the scheme to usurp him.

PLAINVIEW

Perched on foot rails of Pénjamo's Bar,
black hair slicked Borrego kids slowly
flip grit through the open door.
Gazing out to prairie sea
at lizards wolfing gnats,
at tumbleweeds stilled by windlock,
they outline mountain ridges with bald eyes.

A hairy sprocket drops pretzels—
two small bags. The children eat
gazing out to prairie sea
at shimmering heat waves
at moving mountains
sealing eyes
noon red

MOCTEZUMA'S TREASURE

Go
   Went
         Gone
How did it happen?
We did better, at times,
than keep the commandments.
Each day was holy to us.
Our parents were divine.
We coveted nothing
      except our appointed tongue.

One hundred years ago
we would not have
entered crypts
without a burning lamp
or traded lands for candles
and a coffin
      or declined strange verbs.

Yet we descend
marble steps to a corridor
where there are swishings
of other robes and odd tongues,
where, in the anti-room
we will be asked, again,
      of Moctezuma's treasure.

MIRANDO AQUELLOS DESDE LOS CAMPOS

"Copulation is a dangerous pastime."
—Prologue, *The Sorrows of Priapus,*
by Edward Dahlberg

Yes, one bed, one wife—
Too much and so too little—
for esos propagators intertwined
at the rising of the Dogstar.

Yes, the marriage beds
and wives wither, and
yes, husbands boar their heads
and divining rods through
boarhouses and vomitoriums
yes, whoremonging,
craving, divining ruin.

Yet
Has the taste for testicles—
one's own or his compa's—
ever been otherwise?

Y los chicanos—
¿Se quieren visitar
los mismos lugares?
¿Emplear los mismos
pleasures amatorios?

Qué bueno
que se apuran entonces,
porque querríamos preparar
los coffins hoy día
for your senile carcasses,
forty years old and worming.

UNATTENDED

Unattended, it is a small
matter to post oneself
before the unlocked door
to Zion, smaller than
boarding xebecs to Greece.

The back door, a bastard's
entrance, is monitored
by Cerberus who excludes
entrance even to janitors
who wish only to clean
the fouled tombs of
ancestors so that inscriptions
of Tlaloc may be seen.

Since, it seems, the doors
of tombs remain unwashed,
rains from unknown skies
will swirl from all directions
and spit us, one after another,
upon the jaded slabs
to read until our eyes bald
of our own vection,
until our own small vessels
duct toward veneration.

GIRDED US

Aged escapists reflux
arthritic currents
drowning out the
luxury of an alley;
ubiquitous garbage
collectors chant
fat futures and
we're swimming
in a barrel up to
our ying-yangs in dung.

Chaff

PICO BLANCO

On your "steep sea-wave of marble,"
I stand—mad Cassandra, screeching
perhaps, but straining my eyes
to catch a glimpse of the "great king,
cold and austere," or the "pale
hunchback shuffling along corridors,"
or Azevedo's three giant Indians
stepping over the Ventana Mountains.
These are the stewards of *your* estate.
You will, I hope, entertain the blond
harlot while I search for mine.
Never mind cousin Christ. He will
rise above America's adoration for
blood in the corners.

"Poor bitch," you say. Indeed I am,
but I am not mumbling to my people
or to my gods. I am chipping the
crust of the Pico Blanco.
Your stewards could help—or you,
Jeffers; then you and I could vacillate
breaking the crust—You and I, Jeffers.

MARTHA

Martha's favorite phrase was,
"He doesn't know shit from Shinola.
Moreover, you don't know
shit from Shinola.
Moreover, she . . . ," and I sat
in awe, absorbing the moreovers
and shining her shoes.

WITHOUT BARK

after Hesse

If the trees in the background
remain sombre, let it be.
Let the background exist
in the ephemeral realm
that is forbidden to us
who curse the broken,
splintered branches.
Year after year even
broken branches rattle
songs in the wind.
Let them rattle one
more summer, one more
long winter.

LET THE GIANTS CACKLE

Words, words, English words—
turds of the golden goose—
words we picked up, wiped off,
cleaned up, prepared and served
as canapés to the lordly lords
that they might digest—again—
their famished thoughts
to fart their foul days away
                beanfeasting.

RE: AN EGYPTIAN KING

Embraced by an elm
Cooled by its shade
We sat beneath
To discuss severance
And its disorder,
Stasis with its
Non-order, and
I-Thou as the garden balm;
We excuse annoying flies
Crawling on our arms and legs
Daring to defecate
On a knee, a hand, a breast.
Maddening noise from their wings
Thrusts you into Nun;
I grope for your hand,
Utter "My Lord!"
And seize the finger of Atum
As one fly alights on another,
In the crevice of dry bark.

ORANGETHROATS

Bolting gurgles within me
Resound the heavy heave of
An aquarium in the room across.
Torn fin swills are half-sucked
By vacuum. The process of breeding
Forces eggs into the umbraed bin
Swishing, swishing, swishing.

I witness orangethroats breeding,
Feeding deposits with the tide,
Burying proof of spawning
Burying proof that the faucet drips,
Plotting vapor lakes in a dish
Bolting gurgles within me.

PLUMB

Before we ate
While I was putting
The snow shovel away,
I saw two robins.

The enchiladas and
Apple cider washed
Easily with our
Conversation down.

From the window
I studied the robins
Keeping each other warm
While you instructed
Me in Hemingway;

It was a fine day for learning.

A TROPEZONES EN STANFORD

Anoche
los lagartos del desierto

me pidieron canciones.

Ahora—
Mi espíritu sin tono rítmico
trémulo de angustias
Porque—
Ayer me pusieron en el río seco
desnuda hasta los sueños.
Debo hallar las cadenas
de su corriente.
Polvo hallé, polvo y
polvo no más.

Mañana—
me van a descarnar la lengua.

"WHAT SWEET DELIGHT
A QUIET LIFE AFFORDS"

—In Memory of Carol Sue Yarnall

O yes, Cancer child,
Adolescent of fountains,
Woman of seas—
Madness, madness
it is to be less
than a legend—
as you,
as your warm soul
moves eternity
with a pulse
we do not know,
as your quiet breath
exiles the wind
to the moon,
as your brief solitude
fills the universe
with sounds of cellos

CHAFF

—for Carol Sue Yarnall

Recreate man, you say?
First I must examine
What form he takes
Before you begin

In your own image, you say?
He is alone and
Wears no clothes
Save for his past.

Recreate, then. I accept.

He does not now smile?
Erase!
Erase!
Bastard, unyielding as before!

So Not to Be Mottled

ANDANDO

From tomb to tomb voy andando,
buscando un punto final
to an age ya mero olvidado.

Cuando en las ruinas del Xlak-pak
hallando un tesoro de oro
explorers are less puzzled

Than I am now on this mountain.
Con el alma del presente
yo sucumbo al pasado

And to the secrets rolling through tall weeds
of my abuelos' mountain. I listen to their
laughter among the field mice.

From tomb to tomb voy andando,
buscando un punto final
to an age ya mero olvidado.

FROM THE VESTIBULE

In all those years in the choir
loft I never understood
the sermons. And now,
excommunicant that I am,
they are very clear to me.

In all those years in the choir
I watched the benediction
and thought of Vesuvius and Pompeii
and magic mountains where I could
sing into crater lakes and cliffside
caves at dusk or dawn or noon.

From the vestibule
I hear a priest weep,
a child cry,
a dog howl,
and all is very clear to me now.

AMONG THE ORDAINED

Miscreants they call us,
those warty toads lost
in basements of their
own ordinance.
Miscreants, yes,
mournful miscreants
whose bones sustain
the structure as it crumbles,
Hellish miscreants
whose hands form gothic
deeds as were designed
by ordinands,
Villainous miscreants
who rape the wrongs
avenging wrongs
wronging miscreants.
They call us miscreants
Yes, miscreants.

GOOD FRIDAY, 1973

These strange and pregnant hours
Are not the silent ones
Of unremitting birth.

On this heavy Friday
People walk quickly and
In time to Jesu bells;
Shopkeepers lock their doors
After customers who
Do not know that noon sounds.

Two who know cough
Their way against the *foule,*
Against the drolling tones.
They and the hours are poles
In which there turns no wheel
No spoke and no bearing
To balance things this day
Good as it is

SONNET, FREELY ADAPTED

—for J. R. S.

Do not ask, sir, why this weary woman
Wears well the compass of gay boys and men.
Masculinity is not manhood's realm
Which falters when ground passions overwhelm.
O, no! It is a gentle, dovelet's wing
That rides the storm and is never broken.
It is whispered, secret words that bring
To breath more hallowed sounds left unspoken.
Men, sir, are not bell hammers between rounds
Within the rings of bloody gloves and games.
Men, sir, ought not rend the mind round square's round,
Spent, rebuked, and trembling in fitted frames.
    So I return, sir, worn, rebuked, and spent
    To gentle femininity content.

AS VIEWED FROM THE TERRACE

As viewed from the terrace
Our choice is between the
    sacred and profane.
Whether to immerse our desires
    in grapes and chains
is one method open to lovers
or to infuse wine, water, and
    blood is another.

The choice is a child's lot,
The child is the lover's.

Suppose we show the world
our little act of unbinding the bound,
unmindful of the mound beneath
lover's leap, and in our act
enact re-acting as the script dictates.

Suppose further that we let
loose the masking tape and
mask off proscenium arches.
Our play will include
fornicating in the orchestra pit
and copulating offstage like desperate mimics.

We will be applauded to be sure;
We will be lauded as true blue
    stars of love and theatre.
We will receive citations for gyrations,
    protection for erection
        facts for acts.

We will be accepted
          respected
               elected
and in the end dejected,
          don't you suppose?

As viewed from the terrace
Our choice is between the sacred and profane
infusing
          desiring
                    choosing—
a child's lot.

"THE EXTRAORDINARY
PATIENCE OF THINGS"

from "Carmel Point"

Pasturing horses blink as the spoiler
steals in next to milch cows. Poppy
and lupine fields, walled in by the
intruder, stoop with the cliffs
crumbling beneath them.

How fortunate that in time all our works
will dissolve, like us, and return to dust
or less than that.

—As for us:
We center our minds on our minds:
We humanize the unhuman and become confident
As the very grain of the granite housing fossils.

WIDOW'S BARTER

I'll let you stay; Your
Web is not so disturbing.
There are enough eight-
Legged creatures here to
Keep you in climax 'til June;

But you must confine your
Entrapments to the crack
Near the sill. Otherwise
I'd have a pressing mess
And I hate funerals.

I like deaths, though;
That is why you'll stay.
You will provide me with
A lifetime of deaths and
The fanning of eight wiggly legs
on hot nights.

SO NOT TO BE MOTTLED

You insult me
When you say I'm
Schizophrenic.
My divisions are
Infinite.

Situation

DERBY

He whipped his horses
To an incalculable speed
Racing against the undertaker's
Empty hearse-carriage.

PUEBLO WINTER

Sparrows in Pueblo perch on empty
elm branches cocking their heads
at each other or at each shadow
under the warming winter sun.

They watch each other watch
each other and seem, at times,
more passive than their shadows
under the warming winter sun

until a robin flights by to break
their bobbing trance. Another robin
joins the first. Both alight
on a chokeberry bush

scattering the flapping
sparrows to the pole lines above.
From the lines they watch
the robins on the cherry bush.

One robin pecks at a drying cherry
while the silent other lays witness
to the act; so, too, the sparrows
under the warming sun.

41 TRINKETS

The Navajo Indian
knows our god;
he sells giant pine cones
painted silver, turquoise-
studded rocks and bright
synthetic feathers.
The silent river near his
shop carves such a bend
the Navajo relocates
after each rainfall.

AT HAND

Pinched
By a flusher
Handle of an
Old-fashioned john
He sucked a swelling
Finger to
Channel the blood
Homeward.

ANTON CHICO BRIDGE

A mind is such a shallow stream
rippling over pebbles and sediment
on its path toward the desert.
To measure the depth is blasphemy
to the Pecos and to the red clay
of Antón Chico.

> ¿Y qué más queda por decir?
> ¿Y qué más queda por decir?

It avoids deep waters, seeking
its own route to the
Seven Cities of Cíbola,
ravaging its own pathway,
ignoring the earth bleed,
and stops short in Kansas.

> ¿Y qué más queda por decir?
> ¿Y qué más queda por decir?

Under Antón Chico Bridge flows
a deeper, wider mind whose water,
even in its clearest moments,
knows itself to be muddy with adobe.

> ¿Y qué más queda por decir?
> ¿Y qué más queda por decir?

PHANTOM ECLIPSE

It gleams in the morning sun
like a temple on a friendly planet

utter white and looming high—
it stills the spastic eye, the eye

that nightly enters dark corridors
filled with mental lepers' eyes

seeking the sun at the end of a tunnel
searching in the world of eyes,

seeing nothing, nothing.

EL BURRITO CAFE

Through the swinging doors
That lead to your kitchen,
I watch you taste
The menudo you
Prepare for drunks.
Somehow, Augustina
Godínez, the title
Chef does not suit
Your position.

DENIZENS

at the crossroads
a guitarist winks
to the sun
through trees
    then
asks a squatted
beggar
What color are morning reflections?
    aside
each calls the other
    fool

STATE STREET

It is morning
that cradles the
carriage of a
waning Mexican
and his black young bride;
opium and age
gauze his vision from
twisted legs and
fallen arches
of her stumped feet.

Tottering arm-in-arm
the mortal lovers move
toward Mitzey's Bar.

SITUATION

I accept your proposal,
And it doesn't matter
That you are an undertaker.
Do you mind that I am
A midwife?

Restless Serpents

STONE SERPENTS

Stone serpent balustrades line
the castle of the weary wealthy.
Neither the mind, the heart, nor
the soul within move beyond the
concrete and asphalt walkways;
nor can they. The moat from
there to here has not been lowered.
The causeways are filled with the
temple's rusting treasures.

No man within has noticed the carved
serpents of the balustrades, nor has
he looked at the balance of design
upon the stone, nor has he seen what
snatched the life from his sight.
No woman dares to raise her eyes,
her finger, or voice; and no child
or the idea of a child dare be born
to her within the castle of the
weary wealthy. On either side,
stone serpents lie carved into the balustrades.

PROPRIETY, 1972

One evening after
supper dishes were
washed and put away,
Loretta sat in the
back yard next to
Juanito who was
chopping wood.
Fingering blue crystal
rosary beads and
watching Teresa,
the oldest, go into
the outhouse,
she decided to kill
their goat
in the morning.

AND ALL FLOWS PAST

after Roethke

I remember how it was
when my brother drove us in his pickup
truck across Siloam prairie after a late autumn snowstorm.

It was a ride in and out of the self—
romping in four-wheel drive,
seducing frozen cedars to chip off sap, and
searing fence posts to ghostly stumps of lost conifers,
when, fending with the assurance of Absalom,
we raced at eighty miles sideways.

Our unclipped heads searched for
hidden ravines where wheels could get
lodged in pits. Father-rocking traction
would lull us for a throttled charge up
the gorge and jack-knife turn onto the blinding
white sea plain fenced to a mountain.

The snow lay high on cattle
guards where no one yet disturbed
the ridgy silence.

At floor-board urge the truck careened
toward the steel grooved trap cracking
the trend of air beneath the wheels
while our axled bodies climaxed.

Ignoring the mountains' advance, we whip-
lashed toward that hour known
to all darting offspring.

ANGELITA'S UTILITY

It is not enough I am
A child of poverty—
A child among twelve—
A poverty among indigence;
It is not enough I
acknowledge my impotence,
My gainlessness, my
Inutility. I demask
Myself; I disrobe;
I rest prostrate.

I can live this way—
Let me live this way.
Prostrate I can taste
The ground I disgrace;
Naked I can feel the
Confusion I caused;
Unmasked I can see
My pockmarked belly
Grow to explosion.
Let me die this way.

BLEATING

A greater reflection
of the black mirror
haunts me to pray
for an existence
on edge with
any other.

Cliff-hanging
though, is not
the way to lay
me down to
reach the top
of Adam's heap.

Nor is brick laying
to my liking—stacking
Babel skyscrapers
(out of desperation)
toward arbitrary clouds.

I yearn instead
for goat's milk,
piñons, and the
absence of color
in this painted corner.

METAPHOR AND REALITY

Working in canneries or
picking beets is the
metaphor of being,
of being as it has been
in the scheme of things.

As it is, the dream remains
for you who sit easily with
Grendel and Godzilla
as they pick their teeth
with your children's bones.

SIN TITULO

What if we survive?

A LITANY FOR MAD MASTERS

Smell the grand painting on the wall.
It is milk color and feces scent,
painted by a crowning woman
who kept falling through
the wedge of sheeted beds.

Falling, crawling back over rocks
around cliffs, and through the
plotting maps of coastlands,
edging her waning form
against the cliff and fondling its walls,
she bellowed like the bloated cows above.

"Milk them! Milk them!" she cried,
caressing the cornered wall feverishly.
The cows mooed and she blinked
and the cows moved away.

Small and limp she rounded her sobbing frame
to fill the corner. It throbbed like subwaves
in silent caves, throbbing her form full,
reeling it 'til the cows returned.

Moving mutely she searched then felt the
warm cluster, watching the cows, ever watching
through the corner of her eye.
"Moo," they said. "Who?" she said. "Moo," they said.

Shunning the lashing waves, she stirred
her medium gift and started painting
moon beaches and sinking cliffs
as the cows moved once again
above the wall.

RESTLESS SERPENTS

The duty of a cobra's master
is fraught with fettered chores.

Spite strikes the
humbling stroke of
neglect—coiling,
recoiling, pricking
the master's veins
of lapse, draining
a bounded resurrection
to numb the drumming
pain. Lyrics,
lyrics alone soothe
restless serpents.

From all corners
precision humming
and rhythmic sounds
fill the mindful
master who laps
about the droppings
of disregard. Lyrics,
lyrics alone soothe
restless serpents, strokes
more devastating than
devastation arrived.

And Everything Will Perish

SHEEN

I

A yellow butterfly
Flies over the graves
Along the wooden fence.
It will not leave.
A man in a yellow
Sport jacket bicycles by
And I am stunned by the sense
Of this brief moment of yellowness.

II

Three hours the yellow butterfly lingers;
Three hours the man circles
Through the cemetery cycling;

Two conscious movements in the cemetery
Unconsciously charming me at my window
Singing and grieving in the same hue.

III

Our world is made Solful here.
Song in the Mission Cemetery
Is marauding death's mission.

I chronicle the mission, the three
Trajectories, our shared silence,
Floating above the circled graves.

ENDURANCE

A pregnant woman strolls leisurely
through the cemetery lanes.
She heads toward the section
called Babyland where mothers
have propped teddy bears against
the tombstones. I am helpless
to call her back,
but back she comes, clutching
her arms; a shawl hanging
from her elbow, bobs a
quicker pace. She heads toward
the open gate where a chain commands.

VELOCITY TREBLED

The piercing shrill and speed of silence
Augmented one thousand times
Reach a redness to this eye for sound.
How is the point where sound disappears reached?

I have heard scintillating fragments of silence
As memory increases and madness fades.

Mazes of dimensions unspaced, light an ear's
　　　　slanted pathway.
Molecules spatter,
Assuredly,
Dimensions divide, unaffected by my inquiry.
And,
Solids liquify, condescending passage
Of the sun's order. Yes.
Water solidifies
Holding the plan at bay.
Am I to assume . . . yes,
This is the speed of silence?

ZONES UNKNOWN

Snow- and ice-clad, the vessel
Sailed, diagonally
From us, travellers into
The unknown. We watched the sail
Disappear into the void,
Light streaming directionless.
Passengers abandoned, we
Gazed, enraptured: A vessel
moving across the light field.
A vehicle of Sailors,
Leaving a horizontal
Imprint, a focus for our
Last glimpse of who we once were.

This, the record of an act
Of abandonment in zones
Unknown, and too cold to be
Comforting, is my comfort.

My companion sleeps for now.
Incomprehension grips me.
I must retrace our journey
Here to this Center of God's
Abandoned. There are others
Here, too, I sense their presence,
Or their storming, unstilled selves.
They are my unknown future,
And I must recall the past.

LUCIANO

From the south coast I watched,
or tried to watch, this month's lunar eclipse.
Instead, a vision of Uncle Luciano
lying in a muddy street, looking at the moon,
appeared at 3:30 a.m. The eclipse was all
he wanted to see, he said, shaking
a liquid prism before my eyes.

When he was alive, he was a man of extraordinary traits:
        unhappiness
        integrity
        silence
        devotion.
He was a farmer, a coal miner and then a gravedigger.
A look of permanent shock stocked his face, stooped his
                           frame.
Life had lied to him and the truth he bore of that,
bored him into the ground, ground him into a silence,
silenced him with comprehension and incomprehension,
daily, to the end.

AFTER IMAGE

A field, empty, vast—
swept clean by a wind long gone.

To my left stands a steel flagpole.
A limp flag is at half-mast.

The ropes against the pole
clang and clang.

NATURAL RITES

I imagined the measure of love
as the measure of beauty;
that it was unrelated
to the sewers of Venice;
that it complied somehow
to movements of wheat fields,
mountain eagles, and northern gazelles.

I did not phantom its horrors—
Faustian failures in vineyards,
Divine betrayals sealed to drunken hours,
The mark of beasts upon the breast.

I cower before the obstinacies.

GRINGOS

Odin, their god who forgets them
each time the wind changes, whistles.
They must depend on crabs for guidance.
Money changers are their priests.
Their priests conspire with wine merchants.
Odin favors wine merchants.
All others are heretics.

The wind's change, changes the tide.
The heretics do not all drown
during the shift. The vineyards
will not receive rain this season.
The rains have elected to join the wind
to keep Odin on key.

LETTER

If a letter is needed
to set the universe into new
tremors, may that letter, too,
be written anonymously, and
may it be ambiguously rude
as well, to set into motion
a new fury among the priests,
                    popes and poets.
None other particularly concern themselves
beyond the word, the letter.

AWAITING GRACE

Like a wolf's howl
repeating fear
before the moon,
the foghorn howls
itself alive
this night moving
its heaving breath.
Behind the fog's crawl,
I imagine moans,
the moon's fullness waning.
It is a night
to imagine
to lie awake
and watch fear crawl,
drag its belly,
mark women
oddly, early
in the rocky mind.
Awaiting its chill,
I envision death.
I imagine
one newborn thought
of one woman
awaiting grace,
an angel's visit,
annunciation,
a star in the East.

MISTRAL

From some other planet's sublime past
come the terrors that make us prophesize
the end of this year's agonies,
year after year. We mock the prophets
for our silly sense of time and terror,
terrorizing them into lashing silences
against cliffs darker than lava lakes:

Winds leafing through our pliable lives
cleanse our hearing instruments,
dry our fears on the prophet's cliffs
and subdue our gnashings after our own livers.

STEARN WHARF

Wind shifts.
Nearby, a child sneezes.
Sea gulls fly in place.
A lone man rows his boat back.
Waves move southerly
the motherly move,
warm in winter.
Lone man, like war,
is useless to the moment's shift.

The sun's sparkles, scattered,
blown clear for the pelican's glide.
Motorboats are quickly coming in port.
In the distance, mists are making
　　　　　islands disappear.

PAVILION

Returning home before sunrise,
the followers of false freedoms,
the outpatients of religion's pavilion—
all learned the way home by belly crawl.
On the way, we learned the study of flames,
the angle of ascent, the decline of desire;
we lived the poverty of images
imagining a future, anticipating spectacle
with the patience of trees; and
we imposed our presence on the ailing,
friends reluctant to embrace deterioration.
We the vanished lived randomly,
        finally
        the sun's flight
        returns
        a silent shift.

GOOD FRIDAY, 1984

The soldier yields his secret
in his deliberate stride
garnished by quick glances
to the edge of the path
just taken.

His unutterable love,
shielded by weakness ablaze,
exposed like ghouls in exile,
submitted, like vertical glaciers,
to the season of sacrifice.

Unarmed, he fears
his own resurrection
his love for Mary Magdalene
his own summons to act.

THE WARMER CLIMATE

A confrontation between such silence
and mediocre mouthing takes no form,
unless eventual erosion of the soul
can be claimed; still, chicks within the nest
beg for insects or worms; still, stiff-winged
angels glide by these cliffs
and conspire to measure my sea-whipped throne.

Poorly able to tolerate the silence,
I argue with God in spite of his name.
Stones on the beach below have more reverence.
A short distance into the caves
angels tremble at such arrogance.
But the violent silence has carved a nest
on the ledge of the lower heart valve,
and hardened it as the warmer climate
              of Nature determined.

SUNDAY'S FAITH

—R.P.

Mejor dicho,
¿Qué será lo que quiere el gringo?

We know he requires barbed wire fences,
inactive priests and volcanos,
a loaf of bread, a jug of clean well water
untouched by his own people especially,
and a god to whom he could complain without end.

And without end, he builds fences,
                ordains urban chemists,
                ignores the volcano's rumbles,
                stores his wheat and eats
                his neighbor's pita,
                drinks domestic wines
                with Sunday's faith,
                absolves his people
and complains when God sleeps with his enemy.
Mami,
¿Qué será lo que quiere el gringo?

ANCIENT KNOWLEDGE

—D.K.

The ancient owl and worn hawk
beating wings before a woman
praying in the moonlight by
the side of a stream mean
to sink the woman (secretly named.

They beat their wings
to muffle prayers (unacknowledged
to silence tears (long sought
to fan the fog (disguised
to shroud the night's silence
                (whose song is unheard.

The beating of wings
the beating of women
Ancient art.
Weary.

ONE THOUSAND DEATHS

—A.D.

A man burned one thousand deaths,
Forged lightning forged the fire's edge.
All witches are warned:
Golden, Honey, Amber pale before the new fire.
A man wed to lightning of his/blood
     rescues birds
      crystallized in salt air.

His new bride restores life to
  match one thousand deaths,
    purifies the air, and
      calms the birds.

RECOUNTING THE DAY
June 1, 1984

A day of double love:
two friends appeared
as promised, as needed.

I shall recount someday
the cause of history
the horror of its final lie

Of what I knew and did not know
together with my friends,
one hour's joy and one noon's purge

Of our sorrows eclipsed by our race
our race eclipsed by our small spot in books.

I kissed her. I kissed him.
I kiss this day.

RECOUNTING THE DAY
June 3, 1984

At the end of a tattered day,
I meant to die sometime between
a nap and sunset. But
the doorbell clanged.

A breath from the abyss swept
through the peephole (Fate does
not respect my solitude), and I
dashed divinity aside for a child:

Manuel, el poeta Quetzalcoatl moderno,
Handed me a poem to read, "Cien años de Stanford,"
while he returned to his car for his son.
The poem, on blue paper, was an invitation
to his departure. The winds from the battlements
were scattering poets now, and he wanted
to celebrate the scattering.

I held the beautiful baby.
Café amaretto, gurgled giggles,
Manuel's good fortune, tears
tendered the wound of this sweet hour.
Only the living child did not cry.

RECOUNTING THE DAY

June 5, 1984

I

MENLO PARK

Only the black man knows,
intimately knows the truth,
its equalizing pain, its human dimension
and its power to diminish.
I voted for that and Rev. Jackson.

II

EL CENTRO CHICANO
STANFORD UNIVERSITY

Two women, two men, poets,
strumming their finer souls.
Juan Carlos would envy Chicanos:
Wine. Grapes. Figs. Dates.
Cheese. Mints. And children.
El Centro's walls again
embrace us all, conceal our triumphs, our ardor.
The poets strummed and strummed.

RECOUNTING THE DAY
June 6, 1984

I

It was mostly cold, mostly.
Rain came sporadically.
Soup, an apple and heated wine
on such a day made
Wayne more loving
in his instruction.
When he clasped my hand
with both of his,
I was warmed beyond relief.

II

A book of numbers arrived.
I read once that even odd numbers
have a loving relationship
one three with another three
one seven to another seven
even one to zero.

RECOUNTING THE DAY
June 11, 1984

No fear was exhibited then.
Even white men believed in liberation
for the rest of us in those noble home
days of the Vietnam War.

Now Hitler's laws are reinstated.
The man, Aryan, and ever too ignorant
for human progress, his own included,
smokes a smug cigar, plots spacial war,
and distributes among middle-class
children more cocaine. He is step-
by-club-footed step legislating ignorance,
monolingualism and a Doberman pinscher
in every garage, pistols in every desk drawer.
He is today's one-fingered expert at the computer,
a red telephone at his elbow, an Eva Braun
at his feet. *He* bears no children and
readily condemns those of his own armies
to wheelchairs, at puberty,
for generations. No abortions now in the
evil empire, but abortions eventually.

RECOUNTING THE DAY
June 12, 1984

The Supreme Court ruled the house divided today
in favor of men and paranoia.
Human regression invades and plunders
the white man's house
irretrievably divided now.

We can expect a majority—
the *true* majority—ruling
in favor of lighting fire to that house.

RECOUNTING THE DAY

June 17, 1984

To see a daughter off
to join the warring world
is to see tombs opened and filed
into the future's failing memory;
to see history's mothers
hanging by one centered nail
on cross after Roman cross;
to measure rectangular holes;
wombs of reluctant slopes;
silent to the molten core;
and to shriek the tongueless shriek
of white peacocks aimlessly searching
for substance in this beautiful emptiness.

(Of subordinate news to poets:
it is Father's Day, Graduation Day
at some universities, Trinity Sunday
and the eve of the anniversary of
England's defeat by Jeanne d'Arc.)
Sound the bells.
Joyful newlyweds heed no trail of blood
nor veiled pain which surrounds
the crypt of caged women.
Sound the bells. Drown out the rattling.

ONE MORE POEM FOR ROBERTO

Reverently,
   That is how he reproaches
   us who are so long unloved,
As if he understood
   Yet escaped love's
   sacred, unrelenting need.
Like the sea's winds against
   a stolid tree uprooted,
   he reassured saplings
That in the battle against the wind,
   the wind must come
   to us.

NOON

Water falls in an incomplete red circle
into a tiered reflection pond.
The sound of water falling
muffles the tower bell chimes.

My own shadow shades the images of Roberto.
A certain silence enters inward
          to that room designed for him,
          to that sacred place where birds repine,
          to that structure with no walls to bind
          to that round tower within
          where the belfry hails new winds
          and patterns flights for caged birds,
          where unchecked women amble
          in and out untouched,
          where spoilt men retreat
          to heal their vagrant hearts,
          where love of widows is returned
          by more that spirit whispers
or sounds of water falling in incomplete circles.

UPWARD

I will fulfill the law
    of the universe
    as does the leaf falling
    in sweeps of orange
    and red and yellow,
    curled upward at the edge.

ROBERTO'S DEPARTURE

He left Saturday
heading south, South America, forever, he said.
Illness for two weeks before
wrenched objections from me.
Nonetheless, he left quietly.
It was the morning of the full moon.

Moon crazed, I resumed
routine wrestling with idols,
spent Sunday sleeping
in bitterness and rage
against moons, those full-faced
reflections tossed against
my future's window. Monday,
I concocted a draught for distraction.
Without tasting death, I drank the joke
wildly for unfrowning effect. Bam!
Like that. Just that. That that I did
pickaxed the blow gone south. Sweet sleep
offered me a pen and broke a hold on my story,
      on Roberto's chain.

DEER TRAIL

—for L.D.T.

He retold of the deer trail,
an engulfing darkness of forest trees frozen,
flashing by a blur of speckled eternity,
the flight through the desert of snow,
hour after white hour, fire after fever
until the deer hid, by collective pulse,
in crevices between glistening mountains
which guard us all from armed police.

No food for the deer: twenty-four, forty-eight
hours straight through accustomed road.
Tea and rum for him and his drunken guide.

The ride, fierce and steady to a seeming freedom,
a rich flight enriched by the rhythm of deer pants
hardening in visual stores of breath, altered.
A ride of burning breaths crossed cemetery tombs,
skimmed villages, and avoided monasteries.
Tombstones, civilians from flight; Deer,
warriors of fits force full; The unarmed commandant
survivor, surviving, too, the tale of escape from
rifled police pilfering nature.

Acknowledgments (continued)

Grateful acknowledgment is given to the following publications and organizations that have previously published some of these poems:

Sou'Wester, for "Girded Us" (Winter 1970); *Mosaic*, for "Situation" (February 1971) and "Plumb," "Widow's Barter," and "So Not to Be Mottled" (May 1971); *The Muse*, for "Angelina's Utility," in Vol. 2 (April 1973); *Women's Voices at Stanford*, for "Angelina's Utility" (April 12, 1976); *S/he*, for "Angelina's Utility," in Vol. 1, No. 3 (May 1976); *Expression*, for "Penitents," "Bleating," and "Propriety, 1972," in Vol. 1, No. 2 (July 1974); *Anomie*, for "Re: An Egyptian King"; *La Onda Special Edition: Poetry*, for "Having Drowned," "Sonnet Freely Adapted," and "Litany for Mad Masters," in Vol. 1, No. 9 (April 19, 1975); *Universal*, for "Let the Giants Cackle," in Vol. 2, No. 5 (March 1976); D.C. Heath and Company, for "Penitents," "On Living in Aztlán," "Pico Blanco," and "Restless Serpents," in *The Heath Anthology of American Literature*, eds. Richard Yarborough, et. al. (Lexington, MA: D.C. Heath and Company, 1990); Fondo de Cultura Económica, for "El último baile," "Gata Poem," "A tropezones en Stanford," "Anton Chico Bridge," and "El Burrito Café," in *Chicanos: Antología histórica y literaria*, ed. Tino Villanueva (Mexico: Fondo de Cultura Económica, 1980); Centre de Recherches sur l'Ameríque Anglophone, Université de Bordeaux I, for "Progenitor," "El Burrito Café," and "Restless Serpents," in *Chicano Poetry*, ed. Elyette Andouard-Labarthe (Bordeaux, France: Centre de Recherches sur l'Ameríque Anglophone, Université de Bordeaux I, 1993); Pasigli Editori, for "When We Are Able/Quando riusciremo," "Progenitor/Progenitori," "Pueblo, 1950," "Morning After/Il mattino dopo," "Without Bark/Senza scorza," " 'What Sweet Delight a Quiet Life Affords'/'Quale dolce delizia permette una vita quieta', " "Chaff/Beffa," "From the Vestibule/Dal vestibolo," "Sonnet, Freely Adapted/Sonetto, adattato liberamente," " 'The Extraordinary Patience of Things'/'La straordinaria pazienza delle cose,' " "So Not to Be Mottled/Cosi per non essere a due toni," and "Gata Poem/ Gattapoesia," in *Sotto il Quinto Sole: Antologia di poeti chicani*, ed. Franca Bacchiega (Rome, Italy: Pasigli Editori, 1990); Institución Cultural de Cantabria, for "El último baile," "Gata Poem," and "A tropezones en Stanford," in *Peña Labra*, ed. Juan Gutiérrez Martínez-Conde (Santander, Spain: Institución Cultural de Cantabria, 1988); and *Law Educator's Journal*, for "So Not to Be Mottled" (January 17, 1992).